Deep Sleep & Rapid Weight Loss Hypnosis: Beginners Guided & Self-Hypnosis For Burning Fat, Overcoming Insomnia, Deep Relaxation Including Positive Affirmations & Meditations

By Meditation Made Effortless

Copyright © 2020

All rights reserved.

No material in this book is to be utilized, reproduced in any electronic form, including recording, photocopying without permission from the author.

Table of Contents

Introduction 1

Induction 4

Deepener 7

Maintain Sleep Hygiene Script 11

Get Rid of the Thoughts and Sleep Better 15

Eat in Moderation 21

Sugar Addiction 26

Letting Go of Labels/Beliefs 32

Further Weight loss..37

Weight Loss- Getting Leverage. 42

Body Getting back to Good Health 45

Change Personal History 49

Overcome Insomnia 54

Improve Self-Image 59

Insomnia Relaxation...63

Affirmations/Suggestions...68

To the Narrator

The Introduction, Induction, and Deepener should be 30 Min Long

Maintain Sleep Hygiene and Get rid of the thoughts should be 30 Min long
Eat in Moderation should be 15 Min long
Sugar Addiction be 25 Min long
Letting Go of Labels/Beliefs should be 25 min long
Further Weight Loss should be 15 min long
Getting Leverage should be 20 min long
Getting Back to Good Health should be 30 min long
Change Personal History should be 25 min long..
Overcome Insomnia – should be 20 min long
Improving Self Image – should be 20 min long
Insomnia Relaxation should be 15 min long
Affirmations – should be 50 min long

"…" means take a breath while speaking before you continue.

PAUSE (for a few breaths)

LONGER PAUSE (give time to allow the listener time to imagine what you've suggested)

Introduction

Thank you for choosing **Deep Sleep & Rapid Weight Loss Hypnosis audio**...And choosing this audio only means, you have taken a step towards loving yourself even more. Listening to this audio only means you are self-aware of your sleep and weight issues and you want to sleep better and lose weight to be able to feel energetic, positive, and happy. And...hypnosis can get you started on this effortless Deep Sleep and Rapid Weight Loss Journey.

When you are unable to sleep properly or sleep with many awakenings at night, you may feel lethargic, fatigued and irritated the next morning. This also leads to difficulty in concentration and focus.

When you think about the past and worry about the future, which leads to many thoughts when in bed...and it may stop you from falling and staying asleep...

Pause

With changes in the sleep cycle, the body experiences many changes leading to weight gain because lack of sleep leads to changes in hormones that regulate appetite and hunger.

With listening to this audio regularly, you improve the quality of sleep, regularise hormones, and lose weight.

Pause

When you sleep properly, you feel happy and energetic the next day. You are more focused and productive… ultimately leading you to feel motivated and happy. This helps you stay focused and motivated to lose weight and achieve everyday eating and exercise goals to lose weight faster.

So, congratulations on taking this step to overcome sleep and weight issues. Every time you listen to this audio, you get more and more focused on improving the quality of sleep, health, and quality of your life.

I would like you to sit or lay comfortably, where you will not be distracted. Do not listen to this audio when your mind requires your conscious attention.

Pause

Listen to this audio only when you are relaxed and stationary. Please use headphones so that you can focus on the sound of my voice.

Let us start…

Begin recording

Induction

You are now listening to the sound of my voice… and the sound of my voice only …and as you continue to listen to each word I say…you allow yourself to relax more and more.

Pause

I wonder if you could take a deep breath…hold it for a count of 5… and then exhale.

Pause

Let's start now.

Breathe in Deeply…

Pause

Hold for a count of 5

1… 2…3…4…and 5

Now, exhale…

Pause

Once more, take another deep breath...

Breathe in...

Hold for a count of 5 — 1, 2, 3, 4, 5 (slowly)

Now, breathe out...

Pause

Once more, take another deep breath —

Breathe in

Hold for a count of 5 — 1, 2, 3, 4, 5 (slowly)

Now, breathe out

Pause

And, come back to your normal breathing pattern...

Pause

— And, I wonder... if you could simply bring all your focus and attention to the centre of your eye-brows...with your eyes closed...try to look at the centre of your brows and focus on the point between them...that's right.

Pause

In a moment, I am going to talk to that part of you, which is highly creative…the part that knows exactly how to help you imagine or create anything with the help of your mind's eye.

Pause

And… I know you can do it… because everybody can…we all have a creative mind, that has the ability and capability to create and imagine images in our mind.

I know you must have imagined or visualized or day-dreamed many times in your life. And… our creative part helps us imagine and visualize. Isn't it?

With the help of our creative mind, we can visualize, imagine, write, paint, and dream…and I am going to be talking to that part of you today.

Pause

Deepener

Let your creative part take you on a beautiful journey. The journey that will help you involve all your senses and make you feel you wonderful and much calmer.

Pause

And, I wonder, if you could imagine that you have a private beach, and the whole beach is to yourself. No one else comes to this beach because it belongs to you only.

Longer Pause

You look at the water in front, and notice beautiful waves crashing against the seashore. You listen to the sound of the seagulls….That's right…it's so beautiful and calming.

And, as you look at the waters, you notice many shades of blue, perhaps green too.

You notice light blue, turquoise, deep blue, light green, and several other shades of blue, visible vividly under the beautiful crisp Sunshine….

The sound of the water is soothing to your ears and the sea breeze touches your forehead and cheeks as you walk towards the water on the sand.

Pause

You can feel the water around your ankles and the splashes of water as the waves come crashing against the shore. You move forward and feel the water against your legs...it is soothing and calming.. Isn't it?

You stay inside the water and enjoy the water and Sun...feeling relaxed.

You look towards your right...and notice a comfy hammock tied between two poles. And just on the side, you notice a table with your favourite tropical drink.

Pause

You move towards the hammock to lay in it and relax to enjoy the surroundings as you sip the delicious drink.

Longer Pause

And as you continue to enjoy your drink...you notice a kite in the sky...it's colourful and big perhaps...

You look at it...and it starts to come down towards your beach...

And, as I count down from 10 down to 0, you will find the kite coming closer and closer to the sandy beach and with each count down, you are going to go deeper and deeper into a beautiful state of relaxation.

10...the kite is swaying with the wind

9 ....you are feeling even more relaxed

8...it starts to come closer to the beach

7...you can make out its colours

6 ...as it comes closer...it gets bigger...and you relax yourself even more...

5... you are drifting into a relaxed state of mind

4...deeper and deeper

3...even more relaxed

2...it's going to a touch the beach in a moment

1...its fallen on the beach

0...you are beautifully and deeply relaxed.

Maintain Sleep Hygiene Script

Sleep comes to people naturally and it is a normal process for everyone... You used to sleep peacefully when you were a baby. You learnt a process where you could not sleep properly or perhaps woke up many times during the night...

Pause

The time has come to change this pattern and go back to the old self who used to sleep like a baby and enjoy the sleep. And, for this, you may have to learn habits that are important for you to sleep better without any disturbance at night.

Pause

You know the importance of sleep and how deep sleep and good quality sleep can improve the quality of your life. Isn't it?

With better sleep, you are relaxed, energised, positive, and happy that ultimately improves the quality of the relationship with yourself and the quality of your life.

Pause

From today on...you limit your day time naps to 30 minutes and this helps you sleep better at night. If you wish to sleep during the day to feel fresh...you put an alarm in the day for 30 minutes only. You do not resist the sleep, but be disciplined around it and put a 30 minute alarm to feel alert and fresh.

And I wonder if you know the importance of physical exercising in promoting sleep...

You exercise regularly for at least 30 minutes to feel happy, lose weight and to promote sleep. You avoid strenuous workouts post 8 pm.

You avoid stimulants like alcohol and caffeine after 6 pm. Because they make the brain active and stop you from falling asleep...

You avoid eating heavy meals just before going to bed. You finish your food by 8 pm and if at all you feel hungry post that you have a warm glass of milk. Milk promotes sleep whether animal or almond milk.

You maintain a regular bedtime and keep your phone away. You make a habit of writing all your worries in a worry journal...for not more than 10 minutes and when you close that you know you are ready to let go and sleep.

Pause

You take enough Sunlight to regularise the sleep wake cycle.

You make sure that your sleep environment is calming and pleasant...you ensure that the lights are dim with black out curtains.

Longer Pause.

And as you maintain this sleep hygiene everyday...it gets easier and easier for you to fall asleep every night and staying asleep.

You prepare yourself every night...one hour before going to bed...perhaps you drink warm milk, take a warm shower, massage your feet with warm oil, write your worries in worry journal...and keep your phone far away...

With every passing day...you are getting in the habit of maintaining sleep hygiene to improve the quantity and quality of your sleep..

Longer Pause

Get Rid of the Thoughts and Sleep Better

And, I wonder if you can imagine that there is a room somewhere in your mind, a brightly lit room. Perhaps there's a window through… which the sunshine is coming. And… you notice the room to be full of thoughts and with so much light, you can easily see the thoughts on the walls and the ceiling. They are all there on the four walls…when you look at each side.

You notice them as graffiti or posters or banners…

Longer Pause

Perhaps these are the thoughts from the past about the events that have already happened a long time ago…or perhaps from the latest time.

Pause

On the floor you notice thoughts about the future...and these are mere worries that are not really under your control. But somehow you know that these thoughts about the past and future keep you up and stop you from falling asleep on time.

And, you know with so much on the walls and ceiling, you are getting distracted. You cannot peacefully sit and sleep in the room, because it is full of so many things that are keeping you distracted from the present day.

The time has come to change everything in the room so that you are not distracted and you can sit or sleep peacefully...

Because you want to sleep...isn't it?

I know you can do that...because everybody can.

In a moment, you will notice that there is a staircase for you to reach the top of the walls and ceiling easily. And, just on the side of the staircase, you notice a big trash can to put the posters and banners...and on the other side of the staircase...you notice big buckets of black paint...with a big paint brush.

And, with your powerful imagination...you get on the staircase and reach the ceiling and walls to take off the posters and banners of thoughts from past and future...they do not serve any purpose...they only keep you up for long or give you many awakenings at night, making you feel fatigued the next day and also...making you gain weight.

With all this, you have decided to take them off and put them in the trash can. Isn't it?

Start the job, take off the banners, posters, and put them in the trash can.

Longer Pause

And as you do that...you feel some weight has been lifted off your body and you instantly feel relaxed and calm.

Pause

There are no banners and posters on the walls, but some text or graffiti on the walls. These can be taken off by painting the walls black.

Pick up the brush and start painting the walls black...and as you do that...you feel the sense of relaxation and calm taking over all your senses...

You start to feel relaxed and calm...with every paint stroke….

Colour the walls black now.

Longer Pause

The room is now painted black, the window is shut, and there is no light coming in.

You now look at the floor and you notice future worries ….these are the words that make you anxious or worrisome...and these also keep you up at night...or stop you from falling asleep.

You now need to scrub the floor to get rid of all that you see…

There is a bucket of water and soap….with a scrubber…

You now get to the work…and scrub off all that you see on the floor….

With every stroke…you are getting rid of two worries…that's right…

You can clean the floor now….

Longer Pause

The room now looks absolutely clean from all sides…

It's comfy and you are not distracted…

You now allow yourself to count back from 5 down to 0…and with each count down…you will be twice as relaxed and twice as deep.

5…feeling relaxed
4…going deeper and deeper

3...relaxing more and more..
2...entering a deep state of relaxation
1...calmer and deeper

Affirmations for Sleep

I would now like you to repeat the suggestions after me..

It's easier for me to let go every night (4-5 seconds pause)

I close my eyes and paint the room black when I want to sleep (4-5 seconds pause)

With every brush stroke, it's easier for me to let go and drift into a peaceful sleep (4-5 seconds pause)

I feel drowsier when you imagine yourself painting the room black (4-5 seconds pause)

My mind is relaxed and my thoughts slow down as soon as I hit the bed (4-5 seconds pause)

Eat in Moderation

And, I wonder if you can look at your eating habits...and I wonder if you can simply relax and enjoy the lightness of your body and mind...

I wonder if you know that our stomachs are built to take in food that can fit into our palms but we eat more and let it expand so much that it craves for bigger meals, making us eat more calories and making us gain weight.

Pause

We all are born with a natural ability to know when we are full and our bodies give us signals when we know we are full.

But we ignore these signals because we get caught up in talking, eating, watching movies while eating.

Pause

And because we are not mindful of our eating and get busy doing something else along with that…. we pay attention to other things and rarely give attention to our body's signal.

This makes us eat more and we overeat...expanding our stomachs...making us gain weight…looking thicker and chubbier…

And, now is the time to change this… to be able to reach your ideal goal weight, feel lighter, look slimmer, fitter, and confident. Isn't it?

I wonder if you can imagine the recent time when you overate and how you felt..

Go back to that time now…

Pause

And as you are there...imagine and visualise how you are feeling as you overeat...can you feel the palpitations...and the stuffy feelings...and then how do you feel after eating extra?

Perhaps guilty...

And imagine if you continue to overstuff yourself in every meal and continue to feel guilty...how would you see yourself three months from now?

Longer Pause

Get to know your emotional and physical health...is it getting better or deteriorating?

But you won't reach this state...because you are listening to me and this only means that you want to stop this old habit of yours and eat in moderation.

You can program your mind to eat a healthy and right amount of food where you feel full and not eat extra.

And your very powerful subconscious mind knows exactly when to signal you when you have eaten enough. I wonder if you can now go within yourself and ask your mind to alert you when you have eaten enough that is enough for the body for it to survive and thrive.

Longer Pause

And, as you continue to listen to me...with every word I say...and with every word you hear… you allow yourself to note everything that your subconscious mind is telling you.

All the messages that it is giving and the signals that you will know that you have eaten enough...you know now. And you will listen to this signal...and the message given to you by your subconscious mind. You are now being aware of the signal consciously and subconsciously and this reminds you to stop eating.

Longer Pause

The more you listen to it, the better control you have on this habit and it gets effortless and easier for you to lose weight.

Affirmations/Suggestions

Repeat the below suggestions in your mind after me...

I am aware of the signal to stop eating when I have eaten enough (4-5 seconds pause)

I stop eating when I get the signal (4-5 seconds pause)

I eat mindfully (4-5 seconds pause)

I chew my food at least 10 times in my mouth (4-5 seconds pause)

I relish all the tastes and flavours of each mouthful (4-5 seconds pause)

I love myself and with every passing day I am getting slimmer and slimmer (4-5 seconds pause)

Sugar Addiction

You are listening to me because you are aware of the positive effects of weight loss and you want to achieve the target weight goal. Isn't it?

And one of the ways to promote weight loss and lose weight faster is to give up on sugar. Sugar may make you happy when you have it because it releases dopamine and you want to continue to feel good so you reach the jar of cookies or cakes sitting in the refrigerator more often than required.

Pause

While it makes you happy it has long term effects on your health and you do not want to suffer permanently because something gives you pleasure temporarily. Isn't it?

If you continue to have sugar, it will not only make you gain weight but will affect your mood and brain function. In addition, it will affect your teeth and other organs like kidney, liver, pancreas, and skin.

According to research, the more sugar you eat, the more you will weigh and people who drink sugary beverages tend to weigh more and are at a higher risk of type 2 diabetes. This is because excess amounts of sugar can expand fat cells that releases chemicals leading to weight gain.

And you want to be free and lead a healthy life where you see yourself as slim, fit, and light...isn't it?

And, I wonder if you can imagine or visualise that you are continuing to eat sugar and have sugary drinks for three more months….and I wonder if you can imagine yourself three months from now?

Longer Pause

Have you gained more weight? Look at your legs, stomach, and shoulders...are they looking bulkier. And, now look at yourself six months from now if you continue to have sugary foods and drinks.

Even more bulkier? Look at your teeth and perhaps your skin…

Longer Pause

The good news is that you do not have to face all this because this is when you continue to have sugar but you are listening to me to let go of sugar addiction and this means you will never reach this time in future…and perhaps you will look completely opposite after six months.

Now is the time for you to take control and responsibility for what you do and don't put into your body. You only have this one body and if you damage it for good…you will not be able to pop to the shops and get a new one.

And, now you will change the way you look and think about sugar. And, I want you to fully focus on this experience so that you are able to change the experience and relationship with the sugar.

Pause

Continue to focus on the sound of my voice and the sound of my voice only. And, in the future, you will find sugar disgusting and you no longer want to eat it. The only way to stop having sugar is to completely cut the sugar intake or drinks with added sugar completely.

And listening to this only makes you feel empowered and you know you can reach your ideal goal weight faster if you completely get rid of sugary foods and drinks.

And, I wonder if you can think of your favourite sugary food that you love. And, imagine putting that in your mouth and as you chew it...you know it's getting melted in your mouth and sticking to your teeth and tongue...and you can feel the layer of scum on your teeth, which starts to decay them...and your teeth feel unhappy and sick.

Pause

You feel like getting rid of it...but it is difficult to do so...it just can't come off...and then some of it gets stuck in your saliva...and perhaps... because of stickiness...you also feel a strand of hair and I don't know whose hair is it...but you can feel it ...mixed up with that...and it's in your throat...and you can't get rid of it...and it is making you choke and gag...and you are truly disgusted.

And, you choke and gag...and in a moment...and you can taste sugar, someone's hair...and the choking feeling...

And, I am going to count down from 5 down 0...with each count down...the choking feeling, taste, and the thought of hair...would fade...with each count down.

5, 4, 3, 2, 1, 0....

5...the feeling and taste are diminishing

4...it's fading
3...you are feeling comfortable
2...you are relaxed..
1...you are giving up sugar...
0...you have given up sugar..

And now, every time you see your favourite sugary stuff, you know that eating that will give you the same feelings of choking, gaging, the thought of someone's hair will come in your mind...and you will stop and distract your mind to something else. Perhaps to natural sugars...found in fruits.

Letting Go of Labels/Beliefs

And as you continue to listen to each word I say and continue to go deeper and deeper into a beautiful state of relaxation… I would like you to look within you and look for that place where you have all labels stored. Labels about yourself.

Perhaps the labels that you created or the labels you believed in because others believed in them about you…and those labels that were given to you by others.

Look for those labels…perhaps they are positive and negative.. Perhaps they are compliments or comments…look within yourself and find them now.

Longer Pause

And as you continue to go deeper and deeper, it gets easier to locate them…and I want you to find all the beliefs related to weight loss or weight gain or body…

I know you can do it because everybody can...

And I remember having a conversation with someone I knew who was a therapist and she had a conversation with her father who had a belief that it's difficult to lose weight...and even though he tried all the diets, changed relationship with food, exercised, he could not lose much weight... because the belief or the label he had given to himself was its difficult to lose weight and I cannot lose weight.

And with talking to my friend, he became aware of the limiting belief or label and got rid of it...and then the place it was residing, he filled it up with a positive label or belief that I can lose weight easily... safely...and effortlessly.

Longer Pause

And the real problem was having this belief and I wonder if you have something similar and if yes, then the time has come to get rid of it..

Just imagine getting rid of it …perhaps in the form of a banner or label coming out of your body and reaching a cloud up above… imagine the cloud absorbing it...going millions of millions of miles away…

As it goes up...you feel lighter and lighter...and you know that it's going to be so easy to lose weight with regular exercise and eating right.

And...you fill up the place with a positive label that it's going to be so much easier for you to lose weight now..

Perhaps it's : I lose weight easily or I can lose weight..

Whatever label or belief you want to put yourself in...do that now…

Longer Pause.

And, repeat it five times in your mind….

Longer Pause

That's right...you are now focused and motivated to achieve your ideal goal weight..

Your thoughts, emotions, and actions are working together and harmoniously for you to achieve what you want to achieve...the ideal goal weight...

And, I wonder if you could imagine...yourself three months from now...having achieved a fitter and slimmer body..

What do you notice?

Look at your face, your chest, and your legs...

See how slim you have gotten...and feeling so much lighter and happier...isn't it?

And you can do this and achieve this body knowing and believing that you can lose weight, easily.

You don't try to lose weight...you lose weight.

Affirmations/Suggestions

And, I wonder if you can repeat the following in your mind to strengthen the belief that you are losing weight..

- I am losing weight

- I lose weight easily

- Weight loss is easy

- I can do it

- Every day I am even more motivated to achieve weight loss goals

- I am getting fitter and slimmer

Further Weight loss

You continue to listen to the sound of my voice and the sound of my voice only. And from now on, you will use food only when you are physically hungry and not when you are emotionally or mentally hungry.

You know that food cannot be used in place of an emotion and when you are sad... to feel happy, you substitute happiness with food...and you know that it will only give you negative emotions later, which is guilt or regret.

Do you want to get into that vicious cycle?

Pause

To stay out of the vicious cycle, you always need to make a conscious decision when you are choosing to eat food. Always become aware of the thought and see what it says before you take any action.

You eat to live and to give nutrients to your body and not to give love to your heart or mind.

You eat smaller meals throughout the day...perhaps six smaller meals and exercise regularly to increase the metabolism.

When you are hungry at odd times, you fill yourself up with water based drinks like water or lemonade or black coffee.

You love healthy and nutritious food and look forward to eating meals with plenty of vegetables and fruits. And you plan your meals beforehand so that you know what you are going to eat for each meal. This gives you plenty of energy to move through the day.

Longer Pause

Eating right and exercising also promotes sleep... which in turn promotes weight loss.

And as you continue to achieve goals and you start to notice significant changes in your body shape and weight...with every passing week...

You start to look fitter and better and your clothes fit you even better.

Perhaps with this, you may even think of changing your wardrobe completely with smaller sizes and clothes that are aligned with the latest fashion.

And, I want you to imagine doing that now...Imagine changing your wardrobe with smaller sizes and fashionable clothes.

Longer Pause

With this, you are even more prepared to stay focused on your weight loss journey. You easily say no to sugary and fried foods and say yes to healthy foods with natural sugars.

The more nutritious and healthier foods you eat, the better you feel with every passing day and get excited to plan the meals for the next day.

Pause

And as you continue to plan and eat healthy meals, you can see you are becoming slimmer and more attractive...and perhaps getting ready for a beach holiday.

As soon as you look at the variety of foods, you know what to choose and what to leave. You are easily able to eliminate the foods that make you fat, lousy, lazy, and affect your body weight and skin.

Pause

You choose and pick those foods that make you remember your best body that you want to achieve. The moment you look at healthy foods, you will get an image of you in your mind at your ideal goal weight, wearing attractive clothes.

And it would be easier for you to overlook the unhealthy foods.

Pause

With every passing day, you notice your hair getting better, skin getting better, stomach and thighs getting slimmer and smaller.

And you know you can achieve all this by rejecting all the unhealthy foods and focus on healthy and nutritious foods.

Weight Loss- Getting Leverage.

Now, it is very clear to you...that it takes a certain amount of motivation to make this work. But in order to get the best out of your investment of time and money, there needs to be a lot more of this desire to work towards your goal...

It comes upon you to choose to stop treating your body like an indispensable dumping ground. You see the signs your body is giving you... that it won't put up with this forever. A warning of your unhealthy lifestyles is your tummy. How much longer will it take for you to see these signs?

Over the course of time, we have all suffered the loss of someone. Even though they are gone, we realize that they were an important part of our life... You need to take a look at people who love and care for you...people who hold you dear and rely on you to be there when they need you.

Longer Pause

It is your sole purpose to ensure that they do not suffer the loss of a loved one. It becomes you responsibility to live a healthy, long life with love and respect for your body.... Appreciate the gift of life by choosing to eat healthy, in the right amount and at the right time rather than food that harms you.

Longer Pause

Here I understand that nobody likes being told what to do; so I won't tell you of the dangers you bring upon your life by being overweight...

I won't tell you that overeating greasy food is dangerous and prevents you from having your desired slim, beautiful healthy body.

I will not note down that every fried and sweet food has a high fat and calorie rate that takes away the pleasure of eating it. I would rather just ask you to see yourself if you make the healthy choices and understand how it will make you feel as you make these choices now.

Longer Pause

Body Getting back to Good Health

What do you see when you look yourself in the mirror? Do you see yourself as you are, the real you or it is an image prompted by a chain of thought you built up as a product of your mind conditioning and experiences...

Irrespective of the answer that comes to you now after a deep thought, I am here to let you know that the way you see yourself is going to change for the better...

Pause

It will cleanse and refresh you like a gentle cool breeze only to improve the quality of life. The cobwebs that mask your beauty and your abilities will be blown away.

Your confidence to be able to develop, grow and become stronger by the minute will be brought back into the light.

Let us begin with you focusing on your body. Try to see and understand that your body is nature's miracle. Try to spot a plant or tree that can heal or cause a change in its body by thinking positively.

But the life that you have has given you the ability to cause an effect on your body parts simply by thinking about it, to make it better or worse. You have the ability to earn whatever you set your mind on with a bit of focus.

Notice that when you think of buying a new car, you not only visualize the way it looks but also see how it is being driven around. Your body also has a similar way.

Longer Pause

When something goes wrong, it suddenly doesn't become enough to discard it and think "I don't want this illness anymore . . . " or "I want to stop worrying about my ailments". This only leads to your mind picking up in the positives of these statements, turning and twisting them into "I want this illness." and "I want to worry."

From this moment onwards, start reviewing and censoring any thoughts that come to your mind or any words that come out of your mouth.

Comprehend only the positives and focus on what you wish to achieve. Make sure that every day, you are telling yourself that "My body is returning to natural health" and "My body takes care of me.

You don't realise the numerous functions and skills your body controls unconsciously. These simple functions such as blinking, walking and talking come naturally to you. But the more you think about it the more unfamiliar they begin to feel.

As you focus on these oddities and unfamiliarity, it creates a sense of uneasiness that very soon escalates to paranoia and later causes stress responses from all body parts.

Longer Pause

Grasp the fact that your body takes it upon itself to rejuvenate automatically, and it does this best when you rest and relax.

The more relaxed you feel, the more rest you get, the better it works on its natural functions.

So in the coming week, forget of any problems that you might have and be amazed by the way you feel when you are properly relaxed.

Change Personal History

As you allow yourself to go deeper and deeper, I would like you to know that...

You have the ability to take charge of your life and have full control over it. You are capable and have the ability to be your ideal goal weight in the desired time.

In order to ensure that there is no further relapse, take a look back at your very first attempt and locate the first incident, a comment or any other trigger that caused you to loose belief and confidence in your weight loss journey.

Longer Pause

It might seem to be something insignificant, so as to go unnoticed by you back then. Now, you need to take a closer look and find the root of the problem that changed your entire perspective on any further attempts of your journey to the body you desire.

Once you find and eliminate this issue, nothing stands between you and your determination to succeed.

First, try and locate your most recent experience where you lacked the confidence in your ability to losing weight.

I know you can find it…because everybody can…

Pause

Recollect where you were at this moment, what you were doing and who you were with. Pay attention to anything said or done by you or anyone around you that might have caused this reaction in you.

I want you to put yourself back in that situation and this time offer yourself some kind, encouraging words. Talk to your past self and make them believe in their self. Give them the confidence and the encouragement they lack in order to succeed.

Give them reasons to keep going, not to give up or sabotage any of their efforts. Offer them some comfort, wise words or perhaps a different perspective to change his/her feelings and behaviour.

Pause

Now grab your past self by the shoulders and tell him/her "You can do this.", as you look him/her in the eyes. As you say this, feel it and believe it through every fibre in your body.

And when you are satisfied that you have truly enforced the belief to never give up, move back further into the bridge of time to the next similar event where you lost hope and gave up.

Stand with your past self again; repeat the paragraph to ensure hope and confidence in this event. We will now take a few minutes as you continue to travel to all such points of significant incidences, repairing and reassuring yourself as you make the necessary changes. You need to offer advice and comfort to correct every situation that might have sabotaged your efforts.

Longer Pause

Now visualize a situation in the future where you might stray from your goals. Step into that picture in front of yourself and tell him/her to stop. Coach yourself the way you have in the past. Reason with yourself to stay focused and committed to your goal.

Longer Pause

Do it for this supposed situation and then do it again if you can think of any more situations where you might run off track.

Repeat the reasons to stay strong, believing in your words of encouragement and do not give up unless you have convinced yourself not to drift away from your path to success.

With this, you have moulded a powerful tool in and as yourself. It is okay to make a few mistakes in your journey. A real achievement comes with its ups and downs.

Even an arrow shot to hit the bull's eye trebles in its path as it cuts through air.

Pause

It is fine if you under achieve because as you look back on the long way you've come, you see that you have done well and have come very far and this gives you the courage to keep flying unless you hit the bull's eye.

Overcome Insomnia

And as you continue to listen to each word I say, I wonder if you can imagine a beautiful white fluffy cloud just beneath you...and you notice yourself laying comfortably on it.

In a moment, you notice that it starts to gently drift and you are drifting along with it...

Feeling lighter, calmer, and relaxed...

And this cloud is the depiction of relaxation, comfort, and calmness...

Pause

Every time, you want to sleep...simply imagine drifting away with the cloud....away from the physical world...into a world of relaxation and calmness...

That's right.

And as you continue to listen to me, you allow yourself to drift further and further away...finding yourself to be sleepier and drowsier...

And the more you feel drowsier...the more your body feels relaxed and you go twice as deep into a beautiful state of relaxation...

Pause

You are now comfortably relaxed and your physical body is at rest...

And as you continue to enjoy the beautiful state of relaxation, you notice that this cloud has a special power to absorb every little worry that you may have...that bothers you and stops you from falling asleep..

Pause

The cloud begins to absorb every little worry and as that happens...you notice the cloud becoming heavier and heavier....turns darker and darker...and you begin to feel lighter and lighter...

That's right.

Send all your tensions and worries about your past and future to this large cloud...

It can take all of it in...

Leaving you feeling light and free...

Pause

With every little tension and worry it absorbs, get closer and closer to the sleep….and you can feel the bedding beneath your body…

The comfortable mattress and the bed sheet…and the very comfy pillow…

It is so cosy and relaxing and every time you rest your head on the pillow…you imagine the cloud above your head….and it starts to drift…away into the deepest state of relaxation..

And, you start to give it the day's worries and tension to the cloud…and the cloud takes all of that in…making you feel calmer and free…to help you fall asleep…

Pause

If there are any residual worries…you may imagine the same room with the graffiti, texts, and banner…and you start to paint the walls in black…

And with every stroke of black paint brush…your erase the

graffiti…texts…banners…and the thoughts get painted with black…

The room gets darker and darker…and you feel calmer and calmer…

All the residual thoughts from past and future…

Paint them all..

Longer Pause

And in a moment…I am going to count you down from 10 down to 0…and with each count down…your will be painting the room black…and entering a deep state of relaxation…

10….strokes of paint on the walls…

9…the paint covers the thoughts well…

8…you cannot make out what is behind the paint

7…the room is getting darker..

6…you are thoughtless…

5…you allow yourself to drift further into the state of slumber

4…going further deep

3…drifting even more…

2…becoming even more relaxed

1 …about to sleep

0…deep sleep…

Improve Self-Image

And as you continue to listen to me and allow yourself to drift more and more into a beautiful state of relaxation, I wonder if your mind is open to my suggestions that will have a positive effect on your mind and body.

Pause

You are a great human being with many qualities that your real self is happy, lively, fun, contented...but lately...it all got fogged with eating more...which is inflicting emotional pain.

You know that with eating more you feel guilty and think why did you eat more or eat un-healthy...so you again take actions to eat to feel better...and then feel guilty...this is a never ending vicious cycle...causing you emotional pain.

And…because of this… there is a fog of guilt and other negative thoughts that have stopped you from seeing who you truly are. Isn't it?

I know you are very intelligent and you have the capability to be self-aware…and that is why you are listening to me because you are self-aware of your weight and the goal you want to achieve. That certainly makes you wise and intelligent.

Pause

And, I know you would know that self-love and better appearance come from the states of mind rather than using superficial products to look better. If you believe in yourself and choose not to focus on negative thoughts, you will always want to do better for yourself.

A person who thinks they are ugly or not good enough would always sabotage their efforts to improvise themselves.

If you feel good enough and feel happy, you are in a better frame of mind to achieve weight loss goals and feel the two states of mind – to feel good and look good are always working together harmoniously in your mind.

Pause

So, the better you feel, the better you look and the better you look, the better you feel. Your outside is the reflection of your inside…and better you feel from inside, it is going to reflect on your outside…

And when you see it on your outside and when others see it on your outside…you feel great…you feel appreciated by yourself and others…and then you feel even better…

The more confident you feel, the happier you feel…it's is going to reflect on your body…and you will be even more motivated to achieve your ideal goal weight.

With every passing day, you use your intelligence and be aware of your thoughts…and you choose to focus on the thoughts that make you feel better…and the thoughts that serve no purpose…you simply say "Delete" to those thoughts in your mind…or perhaps show the stop sign to those thoughts…and shift your focus to the positive thoughts…

Longer Pause

And with this, you continue to feel good and continue to look good…and all this reflects on your skin, body, and you stay focused on your weight loss journey.

Insomnia Relaxation

Relaxing your body becomes the first step when you wish to sleep. Let each part of your body relax bit by bit, moving upwards from your toe to your feet, the ankles, the legs, the waist, the chest, the shoulders, your back, arms, hands, throat and then finally your facial muscles….

Pause

As your body relaxes completely, place yourself on a beautiful staircase taking you down to your special place, making you more relaxed, calmer and sleepier.

Keep on counting as you spiral down the stairs and watch everything else dwindle as you reach down to the bottom. Allow your mind to relax in this special, private place. This special place can be envisioned to be anything

- from a tropical beach to a simple beautiful sunset. Imagine a warm, comfortable mist surrounding you and let your mind wander wherever it will go.

Longer Pause

Observe your mind as a distant observer as it pulls out images from your subconscious. Watch these images as they gently and softly drift up floating before you.

Feel yourself floating to a comfortable place with your mind and let yourself feel safe, secure and happy in this relaxing feeling. Sink deeper into wherever your mind takes you as you start feeling sleepier and more relaxed than ever before.

Pause

You are now going to start drifting into a short sleep. For now, imagine a soft mist going into your special place and watch it as it grows thicker, warmer becoming more pleasant and comfortable by the minute.

Pause

As you listen to the sound of my voice allowing this mist to surround you, notice all your thoughts, feelings and memories drifting in and out of your awareness. As the most envelopes your entire self, all of your thoughts, feelings and memories become vague and my voice become more distant, dimming and fading away.

You notice how some vague thoughts and ideas try and enter your consciousness until they finally clear out of your mind with time. Let all these thoughts come up and sit tight as these fade away slowly with my voice.

Hear my sound becoming lower and then disappearing all at once. You now find yourself gliding into a light, comfortable space deep within yourself. You are now going to sleep for a short while as my voice becomes less and less clear. After some time, you are going to hear my voice calling out your name to help you come out of this sleep and return to a comfortable hypnotic rest for a brief time.

Pause

You are now drifting into a deep, diffusing, hazy state of rest; slowly and comfortably falling asleep.

Pause

You have done well. From now onwards, you can drift away into sleep when you wish to. Float into the state of hypnotic rest reaching into your special place. Drain out anything that tenses your body as your body is shrouded by a warm, heavy and comfortable mist.

Any thoughts and memories gliding into your consciousness slowly fade away while you drift into sleep. Sleep for as long as you need to and return back to repeat this process if disturbed at any moment.

Affirmations/Suggestions

1. You nourish your body with healthy food (7 seconds pause)

2. You are full of vitality and energy (7 seconds pause)

3. You love to exercise because it makes you happy (7 seconds pause)

4. You are releasing weight effortlessly (7 seconds pause)

5. You are willing to change (7 seconds pause)

6. You let go of the past easily (7 seconds pause)

7. You are getting energetic with every passing day (7 seconds pause)

8. You pay attention to your sleep (7 seconds pause)

9. I am strong and healthy. (7 seconds pause)

10. You drink at least eight glasses of water everyday (7 seconds pause)

11. You look forward to your daily workout sessions. (7 seconds pause)

12. You listen to the signal and stop when you have eaten enough (7 seconds pause)

13. You are healthy and happy (7 seconds pause)

14. You love to exercise everyday (7 seconds pause)

15. You love to eat fruits and vegetables everyday (7 seconds pause)

16. You are becoming stronger and slimmer with every passing day (7 seconds pause)

17. When you crave sugar, you eat natural foods (7 seconds pause)

18. You are grateful for your health (7 seconds pause)

19. You are practice gratitude everyday (7 seconds pause)

20. You are open to new ways of eating (7 seconds pause)

21. You choose food that make your body stronger and healthier (7 seconds pause)

22. You chew food slowly (7 seconds pause)

23. You relish each mouthful and chew food at least 10 times (7 seconds pause)

24. You are becoming slimmer and lighter every day (7 seconds pause)

25. You love your body and mind (7 seconds pause)

26. You enjoy taking care of your body and mind (7 seconds pause)

27. You maintain sleep hygiene everyday (7 seconds pause)

28. You limit your day time naps to 30 minutes (7 seconds pause)

29. You can do it (7 seconds pause)

30. You are flexible (7 seconds pause)

31. You listen to your body (7 seconds pause)

32. You eat in moderation (7 seconds pause)

33. You eat wholesome foods (7 seconds pause)

34. You leave your past behind (7 seconds pause)

35. You feel decisive and enthusiastic (7 seconds pause)

36. You love your life (7 seconds pause)

37. You set everyday sleep and weight loss goals (7 seconds pause)

38. You take everyday actions to achieve goals (7 seconds pause)

39. You are motivated (7 seconds pause)

40. You focus on the good (7 seconds pause)

41. You are grateful (7 seconds pause)

42. You are happy (7 seconds pause)

43. You are self-aware (7 seconds pause)

44. You love the taste of healthy food (7 seconds pause)

45. You are grateful for the foods that make you healthy (7 seconds pause)

46. All the weights and burdens from the past are melting away (7 seconds pause)

47. You are getting leaner and lighter (7 seconds pause)

48. You are getting fitter and slimmer (7 seconds pause)

49. You see beauty in your body (7 seconds pause)

50. You learn new ways easily (7 seconds pause)

51. Your body is getting healed (7 seconds pause)

52. Everyday you wake up you have feelings of gratitude (7 seconds pause)

53. You trust the process of life (7 seconds pause)

54. You trust yourself and trust your body (7 seconds pause)

55. You love yourself (7 seconds pause)

56. You are compassionate towards yourself (7 seconds pause)

57. You eat mindfully and enjoy every mouthful (7 seconds pause)

58. You are balanced (7 seconds pause)

59. You are competent and capable. (7 seconds pause)

60. You are worthy of love and care (7 seconds pause)

61. You give all the love and care to your own body first (7 seconds pause)

62. You choose positive thoughts (7 seconds pause)

63. You are blessed and abundant (7 seconds pause)

64. You love yourself unconditionally (7 seconds pause)

65. You are complete and whole. (7 seconds pause)

66. You are confident and courageous (7 seconds pause)

67. You forgive yourself for all the past mistakes (7 seconds pause)

68. You stay in present and are more mindful (7 seconds pause)

69. You are confident (7 seconds pause)

70. You have high self esteem (7 seconds pause)

71. You are losing weight every day (7 seconds pause)

72. You are focused on your weight loss journey (7 seconds pause)

73. You pay attention to your food intake (7 seconds pause)

74. You chew your food many times (7 seconds pause)

75. You maintain sleep hygiene (7 seconds pause)

76. You love yourself unconditionally (7 seconds pause)

77. Your body is getting fitter and slimmer (7 seconds pause)

78. You are successful (7 seconds pause)

79. You are confident and motivated (7 seconds pause)

80. You believe in yourself (7 seconds pause)

81. You are good enough (7 seconds pause)

82. You enjoy healthy foods (7 seconds pause)

83. You do pleasurable activities everyday (7 seconds pause)

84. You are intelligent and wise (7 seconds pause)

85. You are lovable, open to receive and give love (7 seconds pause)

86. You enjoy your life (7 seconds pause)

87. You enjoy healthy food (7 seconds pause)

88. You have a beautiful relationship with food and your body (7 seconds pause)

www.ingramcontent.com/pod-product-compliance
Lightning Source LLC
Chambersburg PA
CBHW062147100526
44589CB00014B/1717